THE CHANGING WORLD

MOUNTAINS & VALLEYS

STEVE & JANE PARKER

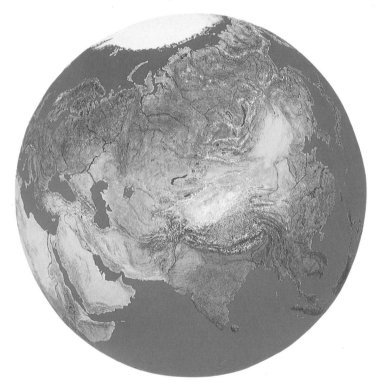

Thunder Bay
P·R·E·S·S

Code of Safety

All activities should be conducted under adult supervision. Most of the habitats described in this series are dangerous because they are at the extremes of how our world works. They are not places you should visit without preparation or without a qualified guide. You should take suitable equipment and wear the right clothing for the environment. Take a map and a compass on all trips and learn how to use them properly. If you should find yourself in such a place through an accident, you will find some tips on how to survive there on page 58.

- **Before you go on a trip**, plan your route. **Always** tell an adult where you are going and when you expect to return.
- **Always go with a friend**, and preferably go as a party of four, which is a safe minimum number.

   If possible, go with at least one adult whom you trust—ideally someone who knows the area and the subject you are studying.
- **Ask permission** before going on to private property.
- **Leave gates closed or open** depending on how you find them. Keep off crops and avoid damaging soils, plants, animals, fences, walls, and gates.
- **Take your litter home** or dispose of it properly.
- **Remember** that many plants and animals, and their homes and habitats, are protected by law.
- **Ask your parents** not to light fires except in an emergency.
- **Beware of natural hazards** such as slippery slopes, crumbling cliffs, loose rocks, rotten tree trunks and branches, soft mud, deep water, swift currents, and tides.
- **Beware of poisonous berries**, plants, and animals: if you are not sure, don't touch them.
- Remember: **if in doubt, always play safe.**

Picture Credits

Susanna Addario: 42/43. Evi Antonio: 54/55. Julian Baker: 24/25; 44/45. Bernard Thornton Artists: (Jim Channell) 10/11, 12/13, 14, 32/33; (George Fryer) 6/7, 8/9, 16/17, 18/19, 30; (Terry Hadler) 20/21, 22/23, 26, 28/29. Bruce Coleman Ltd: 33 (Jules Cowan). Frank Spooner Pictures: 14. Ian Milne: 46. Science Photo Library: back cover, endpapers, 1 (© Tom Van Sant, Geosphere Project, Santa Monica). Wildlife Art Agency: (Wendy Bramell) 36/37; (Robin Budden) 62/63, 64/65; (Robin Carter) 48/49, 59; (Brin Edwards) 52; (Dale Evans) 38/39; (Darren Harvey) 50/51; (Jonathon Potter) 56/57; (Steve Roberts) 34/35; (Mark Stewart) 60/61. Zefa: 11 (Boesch). Activity pictures by Mr Gay Galsworthy.

Thunder Bay Press
5880 Oberlin Drive, Suite 400
San Diego, CA 92121

First published in the United States and Canada by Thunder Bay Press, 1996

Editor	Diana Briscoe
Series Editor	Steve Parker
Designer	Martyn Foote
Art Director	John Strange
Design Assistants	Karen Ferguson
	Victoria Furbisher
DTP Manager	Michael Burgess
Editorial Director	Pippa Rubinstein

Library of Congress Cataloging-in-Publication Data
Parker, Steve.
   Mountains & valleys
   Text by Steve and Jane Parker.
   p.   cm. — (The Changing World)
   Includes index.
   Summary: Looks at how the highest and lowest places on Earth are formed, and discusses climate zones and weather factors for mountains and valleys.
   ISBN 1–57145–026–2
   1. Mountains—Juvenile literature.
   2. Valleys—Juvenile literature.
   [1. Mountains.   2. Valleys.]
I. Parker, Jane, 1951–   II. Title
III. Series: Changing world (San Diego, Calif.)
GB512.P37   1996
551.4'32—dc20
                                        96–5010
                                            CIP
                                            AC

Typeset by Dragon's World Ltd in Garamond, Caslon 540 and Frutiger.
Printed in Italy

Contents

The Changing World of
Mountains and Valleys

Our world, planet Earth, has never been still since it first formed—4,600 million years ago. It goes around the Sun once each year, to bring the changing seasons. It spins like a top once each day, causing the cycle of day and night. Our close companion, the Moon, circles the Earth and produces the rise and fall of the ocean tides. The weather alters endlessly, too. Winds blow, water ripples into waves, clouds drift, rain falls, and storms brew. Land and sea are heated daily by the Sun, and cool or freeze at night.

Living on the Earth, we notice these changes on different time scales. First and fastest is our own experience of passing time, as seconds merge into minutes and hours. We move about, eat and drink, learn and play, rest and sleep. Animals do many of these activities, too.

Second is the longer, slower time scale of months and years. Many plants grow and change over these longer time periods. Return to a natural place after many years, and you see how some of the trees have grown, while others have died and disappeared.

Third is the very long, very slow time scale lasting hundreds, thousands, and millions of years. The Earth itself changes over these immense periods. New mountains thrust up as others wear down. Rivers alter their course. One sea fills with sediments, but huge earth movements and continental drift create another sea elsewhere.

The *CHANGING WORLD* series describes and explains these events—from the immense time span of lands and oceans, to the shorter changes among trees and flowers, to the daily lives of ourselves and other animals. Each book selects one feature or habitat of nature, to reveal in detail. Here you can read how *MOUNTAINS AND VALLEYS* were formed, and how they continue to change today. You can find out about the fascinating plants and animals which live there, from beautiful alpine flowers, to nimble goats, wolves, gorillas, and mountain lions.

4

MORE, AND MORE, AND ...

WORLD POPULATION FIGURES

1 *100,000 years ago—possibly 10 million people—ancient Stone Age*
2 *2,000 years ago—about 200 million people—Roman Empire dominates Europe*
3 *1500—about 420 million people—end of the Middle Ages and the Renaissance; Americas discovered by Europeans*
4 *1850—1,200 million people—the Industrial Revolution is well under way*
5 *1950—2,500 million people—development of intensive farming, antibiotics, other medical care*
6 *2050—projected world population of **11,000 million** people*

In 1995, the world's population was estimated to be 5,760 million people.

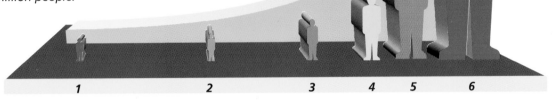

The most numerous large animal on Earth, by many millions, is the human. Our numbers have increased steadily from the start of civilization about 10,000 years ago speeded by advances in public health and hygiene, the Industrial Revolution, gas and diesel engines, better farming, and better medical care.

However, this massive growth in humanity means that almost half the world's people suffer from hunger, poverty, and disease. The animals and plants who share our planet also suffer. As we expand our territory, their natural areas shrink ever faster. We probably destroy one species of plant or animal every week.

However, there is another type of change affecting our world. It is the huge and ever-increasing numbers of humans on the planet. The *CHANGING WORLD* series shows how we have completely altered vast areas—to grow foods, put up homes and other buildings, mine metals and minerals, manufacture goods and gadgets from pencils to washing machines, travel in cars, trains and planes, and generally carry on with our modern lives.

This type of change is causing immense damage.

We take over natural lands and wild places, forcing plants and animals into ever smaller areas. Some of them disappear for ever. We produce all kinds of garbage, waste, poisons, water and air pollution.

However, there is hope. More people are becoming aware of the problems. They want to stop the damage, to save our planet, and to plan for a brighter future. The *CHANGING WORLD* series shows how we can all help. We owe it to our Earth, and to its millions of plants, animals, and other living things, to make a change for the better.

Through the ages, people have looked up at high mountains, their summits hidden above the clouds, in awe and wonder. In Europe, many ancient people thought that high peaks were mystical places with strange powers, and best left alone, since howling winds and driving snow seemed to appear whenever you tackled their slopes.

In Japan, however, some mountains were—and still are—considered as sacred places. In Ancient Greece, Africa, Australia, and many other regions of the world, mountains were believed to be homes of the gods or the original source of humankind.

Few places in the world are completely flat. One quarter of the Earth's land surface is mountainous, and provides us with some of the most spectacular and exciting scenery in the world. When we look up at mountains from the valleys below, we cannot see how huge they really are. The tallest peaks rise nearly 6 miles above sea level. The great forces that create and shape mountains can be even harder to understand—and they are still at work.

Valley to mountain
Death Valley in California is the lowest uncovered point on the Earth's land surface. Most inhabited areas of the world are between 16 and 1,640 feet above sea level, often along sea coasts, rivers and lakes. The highest point on Earth is the summit of Mount Everest, 29,029 feet above sea level— and still rising.

Average land height
1,024 feet

Death Valley
282 feet below sea level

Sea level

Mount Everest *29,029 feet*

Mountains and valleys are the result of the restlessness of our planet's surface (see page 16). The movements are usually so slow that we cannot see them. But young mountains like the Himalayas are still growing taller, by about the length of your thumb, every year. They are 50 million years old, which is young compared to the age of the whole Earth, at around 4,600 million years. Ancient mountains have been in existence for 500 million years or more. They stopped growing long ago.

Measured in the usual way, from sea level up, the world's tallest mountain is Mount Everest in the Himalayas. Second is K2 or Chogori, also in the Himalayan range. But measured from base to summit, both are beaten by Mauna Kea, of the Hawaiian Islands. This volcanic mountain rises 33,474 feet from the seabed. The lowest place is Death Valley in California, 282 feet below sea level.

UNDERWATER MOUNTAINS

Under the sea, there are mountains and valleys, just as on land. In fact, they are even higher and deeper. The tallest seabed mountains break the surface as islands, and the deepest valleys are oceanic trenches that plunge to incredible depths.

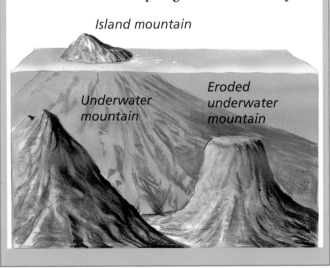

Island mountain

Underwater mountain

Eroded underwater mountain

Down in the Valleys

The general name for the dips, grooves, cracks, and channels in the Earth's surface is valleys. But there are many types of valley, each with its own special feature, such as gorges, canyons, and chasms. Like mountains, valleys are formed by the movements of the outer layer of the Earth, called the crust, and also by the wearing-away effects of wind, water, rain, ice, snow, cold, and the sun's heat.

Some valleys are simply the low parts between mountains. Valleys have also appeared where huge blocks of rock have dropped, leaving higher ones on either side. Where layers of rock, called "strata," have been folded like a concertina, some layers wear away or "erode" more quickly. This leaves rows of ridges, which are hills or mountains, with valleys between them.

River valley
Rivers tend to wear away the land to make a V-shaped valley. This may be deep or shallow, depending on the water flow and the rock's hardness. If the rocks are very hard and the river is narrow, it cuts a canyon or gorge with almost vertical, cliff-like sides.

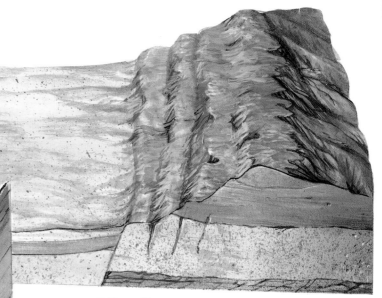

Rift valley
A rift valley is formed when two parts of the Earth's huge, curved surface pull away from each other. The rock block in the middle slips down into the gap or rift. Some of these valleys are more than 62 miles wide and 620 miles long.

Glacial valley
The "river of ice" called a glacier wears away a U-shaped valley with a rounded base. Over tens of thousands of years, as the climate changes, the ice melts to reveal the altered landscape. Gouge marks and dropped boulders show where the glacier once scraped past.

Running water cuts many valleys by wearing long grooves and channels into the rock. The faster the water flows, the deeper and quicker it cuts. The water itself has little effect, but it carries pebbles, stones and boulders that rub, knock, and gouge out the sides and bottom of the river bed. High in the mountains, where the streams roar and tumble at high speed, they may wear out deep holes and gorges. Where rivers flow across flat plains they may gradually wear away a steep-sided canyon.

Ice and snow from high in the mountains flows very slowly downwards, as a glacier. The glaciers are powerful valley-makers. They pick up and carry stones and boulders, which rub and grind away the rocks below and to the sides. The valleys made by rivers and glaciers remain long after the water has gone and the ice has melted. They provide us with good evidence of weather and climate in the past.

Up in the Mountains

The Earth has huge zones of climate, like bands wrapped around it. Around the middle are the tropics, hot all year. To the north and south are temperate lands such as Europe and most of North America, with warm summers and cool winters. Towards the poles, it becomes colder. In the far north or south of the polar lands, temperatures are below freezing for most of the year.

You can see all these conditions without having to walk from the Equator to the Pole—by climbing a mountain. If the mountain is very tall and in a tropical area, then all the world's climate zones can be found between the bottom and the top. Animals and plants from many regions of the world live as close neighbors.

As you climb a mountain, you notice many changes. The atmospheric or air pressure, measured in millibars (mbars), slowly falls—which means that the air gets thinner. This air is usually cleaner and clearer that the air in the valleys below, but it contains less oxygen, which nearly all living things need to survive, so you have to breathe harder.

Height 7,220 feet
Temperature 64°F
Air pressure 820 mbars

Height 3,940 feet
Temperature 75°F
Air pressure 900 mbars

Height 656 feet
Temperature 86°F
Air pressure 1,000 mbars

The plains
Mountain climate zones mimic global climate zones. The climate around the base of the mountain is the same as that in the surrounding area—such as dry savannah, desert, or tropical rainforest.

The foothills
On the lower slopes is a forest zone. It may be deciduous trees that lose their leaves during the cold or dry season, as in Europe and much of North America, or tropical evergreens thriving in high rainfall—a montane (mountain-based) rainforest.

The middle slopes
Next is a conifer zone. This has firs, pines, spruces, and similar cone-bearing trees which are evergreen—they keep their leaves all year round. They are like the forests of northern North America and northern Asia. In Asian areas, this zone may be a forest of bamboo, a giant grass.

Height 17,720 feet
Temperature 32°F
Air pressure 520 mbars

Snow line

Height 9,840 feet
Temperature 57°F
Air pressure 755 mbars

Permanent snow
Near the top, the rocks are always covered by snow and ice. The snow line moves up and down the mountain with the seasons, and some animals follow it in their yearly vertical migrations.

Height 11,480 feet
Temperature 50°F
Air pressure 720 mbars

Tree line

Alpine meadow
Above the tree line, only alpine plants survive. They are low-growing and flower briefly in the short summer. Some large animals visit this level during the warm or wet season.

The snow line also moves with the seasons, rising in summer and falling in winter. Above about 23,000 feet, the air is so thin that there is very little oxygen, and there is little or no liquid water since it is all frozen. So few living things can survive.

The sunshine gets fiercer, especially the ultraviolet rays that cause sunburn. The wind also becomes stronger. Rainfall patterns change as you climb higher. Temperature falls steadily, too, by almost 1° Fahrenheit for every 330 feet of height.

As you go higher and higher, at some stage you reach the place where the temperature is below freezing. This is the snow line. Above it, all water is frozen as ice or snow. Since the starting temperature at the bottom is higher for a tropical mountain than for a temperate one, the snow line on a tropical mountain is higher, too. It is usually about 13,125 feet above sea level, compared to 9,840 or even 6,560 feet on a temperate mountain. In the polar regions of the Arctic and Antarctic, even low hills remain snow-covered.

CLIMBING MOUNTAINS

The first mountain to be climbed officially was Mont Blanc in the European Alps, by Michel Paccard and Jacques Balmat in 1786. Mount Everest was climbed by Edmund Hillary and Tenzing Norgay in 1953. Modern climbers wear very warm, lightweight clothing and use special equipment such as ropes, crampons (boot spikes,) and pitons (ringed spikes to hammer into the rock.)

Mountains and Weather

Prevailing wind
Although the usual winds bring a lot of rain to the windward side of the mountain, it is too high and steep to support much life.

Prevailing winds

Leeward slopes
Water trickles down the flatter slopes, and some rain still falls. So this side of the mountain has trees and other plants, which provide food and homes for animals.

The climate zones up and down the world, and up and down mountains, are caused mainly by the sun. The Equator is warmed most because it is nearer the sun. The Poles are cold because they are farthest from the sun. As the sun warms the land and the air above it, the heated air rises, and cooler air moves along to take its place, producing winds.

Mountains are such huge features in the landscape that they alter the weather around them, even across a whole continent. They can make dry climates wetter and damp climates much drier. As air blows over a mountain, it is forced upwards and so gets cooler. Most air carries moisture as invisible water vapor. As the air cools, the water vapor condenses and becomes tiny water droplets —clouds. The droplets may get bigger and eventually fall as rain.

In the valley
The warm, sheltered valley has plentiful water that has run down from the mountainsides, forming a large river. Conditions for life are good.

This high rainfall produces lush plant life on the lower windward slopes of the mountain, which face the main wind direction. As the wind blows around, over and down the other side of the mountain, it has less moisture. So the leeward slopes of the mountain are usually drier. On the lowlands to the other side, it may be very dry indeed, creating a "rain shadow" desert.

Next mountain
Some moisture is given off into the air from the river, trees, and other wildlife of the valley. When the air rises again, it cools and drops its moisture as rain on the windward slopes of the second mountain. On the far side of this mountain is a dry, barren desert.

13

Mountain Barriers

Mountain ranges form great walls or barriers to animals, plants, people, and even the weather. Animals and plants evolve to fit the different conditions found at different heights on the mountain. They are often so well suited to their own conditions that they cannot survive higher or lower. Since they are unable to cross the climate zones above and below them, they live in isolation, separated by the valleys and lower lands around the mountain. Mountains in their lowlands are like islands in an ocean. Only flying animals—and the tiny seeds of plants that get blown by the wind—can cross mountain chains.

Mountains were once great barriers to people journeying across the land or looking for new places to live. Their size and inhospitable climates were a hindrance to explorers and traders, but a benefit to those trying to keep out invaders. Today, only the tallest mountains are barriers. In most mountains, roads and railways go through tunnels and passes (narrow valleys,) and airplanes fly easily over the peaks, carrying people and goods.

Mountain defense
The head or upper end of a valley is surrounded by steep slopes where few people venture. A town built here could be well defended, since enemies come from one direction only.

The Iceman
Ötzi, as he is known, died about 5,000 years ago trying to cross the Italian Alps. His frozen body was discovered in a glacier in 1991. He wore leather boots stuffed with grass against the cold, fur leggings and jacket, and a grass cloak. He carried an axe, bow and arrows, and equipment for making fire. Why did he set out on such a journey? He may have been a trader, a shepherd looking for lost sheep, or a hunted man fleeing from raiders.

Crossing mountains
A mountain pass is an often steep, wiggly path or track over the lowest point between the peaks. In olden times, whoever guarded the pass controlled travel in the area. Passes were hazardous places, with the risk of ambush and robbery. Today, wide, fast roads are built around the ends of the range, often passing through tunnels in the mountainside.

Higher and Cooler

You can show how the weather conditions change with height, as though you are going up a mountain (see page 10), even without a local mountain. You need a standard maximum–minimum safety thermometer (as used outdoors and in greenhouses) and a toy windmill. Do the activity quickly, to cut down the chances of the weather itself changing.

4 With the help of an adult, do the same experiment on a "mountain," such as a balcony or veranda several stories up, or at a friend's house on higher ground. *Is it even cooler and windier up there?*

1 Choose a dry day when the weather is fairly settled, not too hot or cold, but quite windy. Select a "valley"—a place low down, sheltered, and shaded, such as near the foot of a house wall or yard fence.

2 Put the thermometer here, flat on the ground. Take the temperature after 5 minutes. Hold the windmill to face the wind, and assess the wind speed by how fast it spins.

3 Do the same on a "foothill," such as on top of a fence or wall, but still fairly shaded. *Is it cooler and windier here than in the "valley"?*

The Mini Glacier

Pure ice may be smooth and slippery. But in a glacier it is mixed up with rocks, stones, and other particles, so it scratches and scrapes at the landscape with great power (see page 9). You need some ice-cube trays or bags, a freezer, and a smooth, shiny surface that can be damaged without problems!

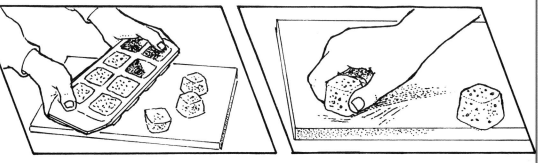

1 Make some ice cubes from faucet water. Make another set with grains of sand in them.
   Rub the pure-water ice cubes on a shiny surface, such as painted or varnished wood. Is there much change?

2 Do the same with the sandy ice cubes. See how the grains work like sandpaper to scratch and gouge. It is a miniature version of a real glacier. The harder you press, the more ice melts and the greater the "erosion."

The Restless Earth

The thin, hard surface of the Earth is called the crust. It is not one huge ball-shaped piece of rock. The crust is made up of gigantic curved jig-saw pieces, called "tectonic plates." These plates drift or float slowly around the globe, driven by the movements of the red-hot, molten rock of the mantle beneath them. The process is sometimes called "continental drift." The crust under the continents or main landmasses is thicker than the crust under the sea. This thinner oceanic crust forms along ridges under the sea, where molten rock from the mantle wells up and goes hard. It gradually spreads outwards from the ridge. In some places it is driven back down into the mantle again as it pushes against the thicker, continental crust.

Different types of mountains and valleys form as a result of the movements of these tectonic plates. Where two unyielding continental plates collide

Mountain ranges of the world

There are two great mountain ranges in the world. One is the Himalayas, Alps, and Atlas mountains stretching across Asia, Europe, and North Africa.

The other is the Rockies and Andes running down the west coasts of North and South America.

Other ranges, like the Appalachians on the East Coast, are much older and worn down by erosion.

Rocky Mountains · Appalachians · Ural Mountains · Altai Mountains · Alps · Pyrenees · Caucasus · Atlas Mountains · Himalayas · East African Highlands · Andes · Snowy Mountains

and push against each other, they wrinkle and buckle into fold mountains. Where the plates pull apart, they leave rift valleys as scars. The edges of the plates may get stuck, and tensions build up. These are released as an earthquake, when the plates slip, creating new ups and downs in the land. Volcanoes are where fiery rocks within the Earth spurt out through weak spots and build mountains.

Mountains and valleys are involved in the continuous cycle of building and destruction that takes place in the Earth's crust, over hundreds of millions of years. Peaks wear down, and valleys fill with the bits. But more earth movements are always raising new mountains and creating new valleys.

Where plates meet
A thin oceanic plate is pushed sideways and slides under a thicker continental plate, to melt back into the mantle below. This is called a "subduction zone." Molten rock oozes up weak spots to form a line of volcanic mountains. A very deep valley, called an oceanic trench, forms under the sea.

Continental plate

Volcanoes

Oceanic trench

Oceanic plate under sea

Mantle

Patterns of Mountains

Cordillera

A mountain cordillera includes various ranges, groups, and systems of mountains, of different origins and ages, arranged together in the same part of a continent. For example, the North American cordillera includes the Rockies, the Cascade range, the Coast ranges, and the Sierra Nevada mountains.

Mountains are made in different ways, as shown on the following pages. They are also arranged in different patterns and formations, which you can see on maps. Single mountains are often volcanic in origin. They build up over weak points in the Earth's crust. Some volcanic mountains form over a site called a hot spot, which stays still as the tectonic plate drifts and slides over it. The result is a row or "chain" of volcanic peaks that get younger, from old and extinct (dead) volcanoes, to new and active ones. An example is the peaks of mountains that form the Hawaiian Islands in the Pacific Ocean.

A mountain "range" is a narrow row or belt of peaks which formed at about the same time, during the same episode of mountain-building—which is known as "orogenesis." Many mountain ranges were made by buckling and folding of the rock layers in the Earth's crust. A cluster of mountains, like the Black Hills in South Dakota, is called a "group."

Several groups and ranges of mountains, which were all caused by the same main process and are all around the same age, are called a mountain "system." One example is the Rocky Mountain system in the western states.

Single peak

This is often formed by a volcano (see pages 22–23). It builds up in layers during each eruption, to form a dome- or cone-shaped mountain. However, this may wear down into other shapes as it becomes older.

Mountain range

The range is a long ridge of peaks, all formed in the same way, usually by folding of the Earth's crust (see pages 20–21). Some ranges are thousands of miles long.

MOUNTAINS ON MAPS

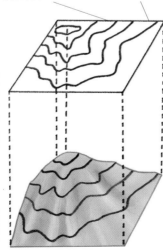

1,000-feet contour

300-feet contour

You can see how mountains and valleys rise and fall on a three-dimensional model of the landscape, but not on a flat two-dimensional map—unless you use contour lines. A contour line joins all places on the land which are at the same altitude (height above sea level.)

The contour lines on a small-scale, detailed map may be at intervals of 100 or 200 feet of altitude. On a large-scale map of a continent, they may represent steps of 1,500 or 3,000 feet in altitude. The closer the contour lines, the steeper the slope. Lots of contour lines almost touching show a nearly vertical cliff.

Fold Mountains

Fold mountains form where the edges of the Earth's great tectonic plates push against each other, as part of the continuing process of continental drift (see page 16). The plate edges buckle and wrinkle into up-and-down ridges. These are tiny compared to the area of the whole tectonic plate, which may be thousands of miles across. But to us, they are huge mountains.

Folds pushed upwards are called "anticlines," and are hills and mountains. Folds that dip down are called "synclines," and are valleys. In some places where the rocks are soft, the folds get worn away by the weather almost as fast as they are pushed up. So proper mountains never form. The folds themselves are shaped into valleys, low hills, or ridges.

The Himalayas are the biggest fold mountains, and the largest mountains in the world. In fact, they contain the twenty-eight tallest peaks, from Everest at 29,029 feet, to Pik Pobedy between

Where folds are found
Most fold mountains are along the edges of the Earth's great tectonic plates. These plates are either pushing towards each other now, or have pushed towards each other in the past. The main ranges are the Himalayas, Andes, Rockies, and European Alps.

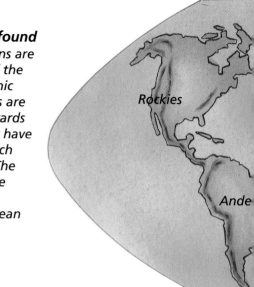

Kirghizia and China at 24,406 feet. The Himalayas started to form about 50 million years ago as the Australian tectonic plate, carrying India, pushed northwards into the Eurasian plate. The surface of the land is still buckling, and the Himalayas are still

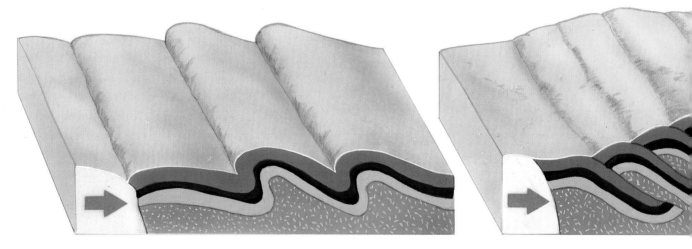

Stage 1
The edges of the tectonic plates push against each other and fold like a accordion. This process usually happens so slowly that the rock sheets bend like cardboard, without cracking.

Stage 2
Sometimes the layers of rocks are split and slide up against each other, in a row of strips. Or they may get bent right over, so the oldest layers of rock are on top.

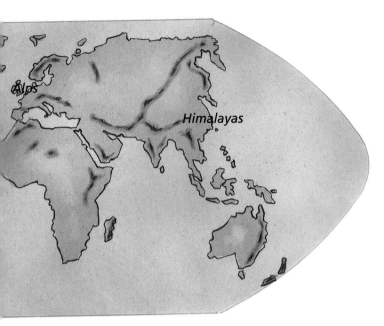

Far in the future, they may look like North America's Appalachian mountains. These are also fold mountains, formed in the same way as the Himalayas, but they are extremely ancient—more than 250 million years old.

The pushing together of the African and Eurasian plates has created three sets of fold mountains. The Urals in Russia are oldest, at about 220 million years. Next come the Pyrenees (between France and Spain), at 200 million years. Youngest are the European Alps—parts of these are only a few million years old. The North America cordillera, including the Rocky Mountains, has been pushed up in different phases from about 160 million years ago to the present.

rising by about 2 inches every year. Their "new" peaks are sharp and angular. Eventually the tectonic plates may change their direction of drifting, and the Himalayas will stop rising. Gradually the processes of erosion will wear them down.

Smaller ridges
The folding and erosion take place on all size scales, so that folds are themselves folded, and so on.

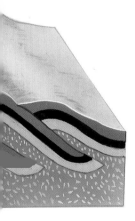

Stage 3
Gradually the forces of erosion smooth out the land. But some rock layers may wear more slowly than others, leaving patterns of ridges and hollows.

Blocks, Faults, and Volcanoes

Some mountains and valleys form where vast cracks, or faults, appear in the Earth's crust. The cracks are caused by huge pressures as the great tectonic plates move past each other. The rocks to the sides of the faults may move up or down in different ways, as shown here. Eventually, the sharp edges of the shifted rock are worn smooth by erosion, and only changes in the pattern of the rock layers, or strata, betray the movement that occurred long ago. Mt. Rundle in New Zealand and the Sierra Nevada mountains in the USA were built by these types of earth movements. Block-fault valleys are called "grabens," and the mountains are called "horsts."

Unlike the incredibly slow movements that produce fold or block-fault mountains, volcanic mountains may appear suddenly and dramatically. Volcanoes form by piling up layers of lava (molten rock) and ash from below the Earth's crust. Kilimanjaro, Africa's tallest peak, was made in this way. The much-smaller Mount Vesuvius in Italy is a cinder cone produced by showers of ash, rather than red-hot lava that cools into solid rock. Ridges and hills, known as "igneous intrusions," (like Stone Mountain in Georgia) are left when molten rock goes solid underground and the overlying layers then wear away.

Sharp edges are worn away

Rise and fall
In one type of block-fault event, a central block of rock slides and sinks down as the lithospheric plates on either side move away from each other. This leaves a rift valley with ridges or peaks on either side (see page 24). In a reverse or thrust fault, the central block is squeezed and pushed up, as the plates on either side push inwards, as shown here.

Plate pushes sideways

Rock layers forced up

Cracks in the world

Block-fault mountains form mainly where the Earth's tectonic plates move past each other. Volcanic mountains form where the crust is too weak to contain the pressure of molten rock below, usually at or near the edges of the plates.

Grampians
Urals
Black Forest
Tien Shan
Sierra Nevada
Asir Mountains
Great Rift Valley & East African highlands
Flinders Range
Great Dividing Range

Displaced layers

The different types of rock show in layers along the sides of the mountain ridge, as they are worn away by the forces of erosion.

HOW A VOLCANO GROWS

The molten rock or "magma" beneath the Earth's crust is under incredible pressure. It may push through a weak point to the surface. The molten rock, now called lava, flows from the opening or vent on to the surface. It cools and goes solid. More lava flows over it at the next eruption. If the lava is thick and cools rapidly, it builds up in layers to make a cone volcano. If the lava is thinner and more runny, it spreads over a wider area, forming a lower, dome-shaped volcano.

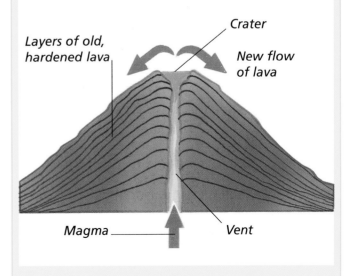

Crater

Layers of old, hardened lava

New flow of lava

Magma

Vent

Grooves in the Land

Where there are mountain peaks, there have to be valleys between them. But valleys, cliffs, and canyons also form in a fairly flat landscape, as gigantic grooves and troughs. Some valleys are worn away over thousands or millions of years by the rushing waters of a river. The river carries boulders and pebbles, which bump and grind away the river bed as they swish downstream. Other valleys are scraped by the very heavy, slow-moving ice of a glacier. The base of the glacier picks up dirt and stones, and gradually gouges deeper into the underlying rocks.

Another type of valley forms when two huge sections of the Earth's surface move apart from each other. (This is part of the general process explained on page 9.) As the sections pull apart, they leave a

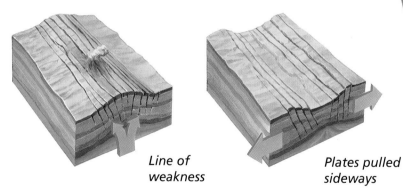

Line of
weakness

Plates pulled
sideways

Rift valley
Two huge plates of the Earth's crust move sideways, as part of the ever-continuing process of continental drift. Volcanoes may erupt along weak points. Cracks or rifts appear, and leave a central block. As the process continues, the central block falls into the widening gap and creates a steep-sided rift valley.

block of land in the middle, which slips down into the trench. This is called a rift valley. Earthquakes can make rift valleys in a few seconds. Then, as time passes, the climate changes, and there are great land movements. The rivers which made the valleys may slowly dry up or flow elsewhere. Or the

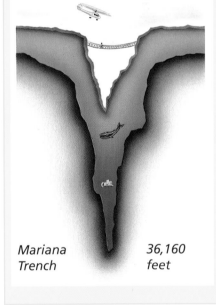

Cracked landscape
Some rift valleys, especially in Africa, stretch for hundreds of miles. Herds of wild animals graze and browse on the valley floor, watched by predators on the valley sides above.

groove-gouging glacier may gradually melt away. Pebbles and soil begin to collect in the lower parts of the valley. When you climb a hill or mountain and look out over the landscape, the valleys may seem shallow and you may not be able to see how they were made. But in other areas, where the landscape is young, the valleys have not yet been filled in and you can see how they were formed.

Erosion

All mountains are eventually eroded, or worn away, by the slow, never-ending forces of the weather. Water attacks the rock in physical and chemical ways. Running water picks up and carries fragments of sand and pebbles. As it flows, it bounces these along the stream bed, and they chip off more fragments that enlarge the channel. Water can also split rocks when it freezes at night or in winter. It seeps into cracks in the rock, and as it turns to ice, it expands and pushes against the crack sides until the rock flakes and breaks. The broken fragments may then be carried away by a glacier—a massive, slowly-flowing ice-river. The endless cycle of heating in the sun by day and cooling at night also cracks and flakes rocks. The chemical carbon dioxide in the air dissolves in raindrops to form a natural weak acid. Modern industrial waste gases also dissolve, forming stronger acids. The acidic rain eats into the rock, dissolving it and washing it away. The wind also plays its part in erosion by sand-blasting rocks and stones to produce spectacular natural sculptures (see page 30).

New,
sharp,
jagged peaks

Towards flatlands
The water, sun, wind, and other forces of nature gradually crack boulders, tumble pebbles, and flake off small particles of rock. The jagged peaks of new mountains are worn lower and smoother over thousands and millions of years. The eroded particles settle in the valleys, filling their lowest parts. But in the future, continuing earth movements will create new peaks and troughs across the land.

Old, rounded, worn-down landscape

Tabletop Mountains

See how fold mountains form (see page 20) with layers of different colors of modeling clay. The real process takes millions of years, but you can do it in only a few seconds!

Make some mini block-fault mountains (see page 22) with blocks of lightweight polystyrene (used for packaging). You also need a modeling knife, water-based paint and an adult to help with the cutting.

1 Roll different-colored lumps of modeling clay into flat, square sheets, each about as thick as your finger. Place the sheets on top of each other, like the layers or strata of rock in the ground.

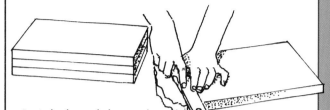

1 Ask the adult to trim the polystyrene into four flat, square sheets about 1 inch thick. **Don't use the knife yourself.** Paint them different colors and hold them together in a pile while wet, so they dry stuck together. These are rock layers.

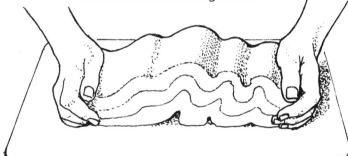

2 The rocks will be squeezed horizontally by the incredible forces of plate tectonics. Do this by pushing together two opposite edges of the rock layers.

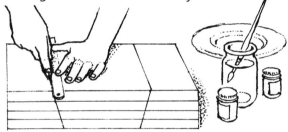

2 Ask the adult to make two cuts in a wide V-shape, as shown. These are fault lines, caused by enormous pressures from drifting plates cracking the Earth's outer crust.

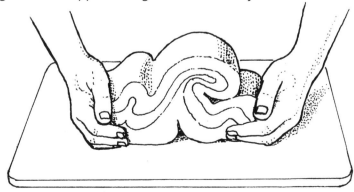

3 As you push, see how the layers begin to bend, buckle, and fold. These are young mountains. Can you get some folds to tip right over, so the layers are upside down?

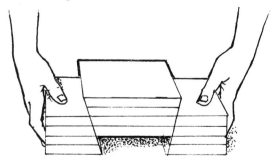

3 Push together the outer portions of polystyrene. See how the central portion is forced up—like a block-fault mountain. If you pull apart the outer portions, can you make a rift valley?

Canyons, Gorges, and Chasms

Rivers are powerful shapers and sculptors of rock. They cut fairly straight V-shaped valleys (see page 9) as they rush steeply down mountain slopes. As the land becomes flatter, their currents slow and the course they wear away is more meandering (wavy) and rounded. The depth of a river valley, the steepness of its sides, and how fast it forms depend on many features. These include the size and speed of the river itself, whether it flows steadily all year or floods in some seasons, how many pebbles, stones, and other particles it carries, and the type and hardness of the rock layers over which it flows.

Canyons form when a deep, steep-sided valley is cut by a river slowly eating its way into a flat plain. The Colorado River has been flowing across the plains of the Southwest for many thousands of

Chasm
Some chasms may not have a permanently flowing stream at their base. They are eroded by chemical action only during sudden flash floods, caused by torrential downpours of rain. For the rest of the time, the chasm bed is dry or has a few deep, shady pools.

THE POWER OF WATER

A gorge forms by successive collapses of a waterfall, as the softer underlying rock is eroded from beneath it. The falling water eats away a deep plunge pool. Then the waterfall moves upstream in a jump as its hard "lip" collapses.

years. It has cut a spectacular valley, the Grand Canyon. The rocks at the top are younger than 200 million years, while those at the bottom are 500 million years old.

Canyon

A canyon is created as a river eats down into a flat plain. The twists and turns of the river, and the canyon it forms, depend on the areas of hardness in the gradually deeper rock layers. In general, the fall of a river is steepest where the rocks are softest.

Hardest, erosion-resistant rocks

Where a river flows over hard rock onto softer rock, a waterfall appears. It drops into a plunge pool where the swirling water cuts back under the topmost, resistant rock layers. The resistant rock is eventually so undercut that it collapses. In this way, a gorge forms. It lengthens by sudden collapses as the waterfall moves upstream. The Niagara River is cutting a gorge as it plunges 165 feet over hard limestone to eat away at the softer shales beneath.

Chasms are deep cracks, clefts or fissures in the land which are cut mainly by the chemical action of acidic water dissolving the limestone rock.

River in flat land

Uplift

A river may wear a shallow valley in a fairly flat plain. But then the land rises because of earth movements, a process called "uplift." The river keeps cutting down, as the land goes up around it. So the river makes a deeper and deeper canyon.

Land rises by uplift

River cuts deeper valley

Canyon forms

Nature's Sculptures

Wherever weathering forces act on rock and stone of different hardnesses, amazing natural sculptures are formed. The hardest rocks of all are igneous rocks like granite. Metamorphic rocks, such as marble and slate, are softer. But the softest of all are the sedimentary rocks, like chalk or sandstone.

Totem poles

In Argentina's Valley of the Moon, in the foothills of the Andes mountains, the wind has sandblasted the rock into tall columns like totem poles with strange faces.

Mushrooms

Strange top-heavy mushrooms of rock near Madrid, Spain, are protected from the rain by roof slabs of hard dolomite rock.

Chimneys and spires

In Monument Valley, Colorado, rivers flowing across the plains for thousands of years have cut many crisscrossing gorges and canyons. Today, only tall chimneys, spires, and mesas are left towering above the new lower-level plains.

Granite tors

Piles of rounded granite blocks, called tors, stand proud on Dartmoor in Britain. They are the result of acidic rainwater eating into cracks in the rock, cutting it into cubes and washing away the loose material to leave it smooth. The tors look like human-made stone stacks.

Ice Power

As water gets colder and freezes into ice, it expands with great pressure. In nature, rain water collects in cracks in the rocks and freezes at night, widening the crack and making the rock surface flake and crumble. You can see this process, called "frost-wedging," using a lump of modeling clay and a deep freezer.

1 Mold the clay into a fist-sized ball. Make some cracks in the surface and dribble water onto them, as though from rain.

2 Put the clay ball into a larger plastic bowl, being careful not to spill the water from the cracks. Place this in a deep freezer overnight.

3 Examine the lump next day. Are the cracks larger? Let the ball thaw, dribble more "rain" onto it, and repeat the overnight freeze. What does the clay ball look like after a few days?

Hard-topped Hills

In some places, blocks of very hard rock protect the softer rock beneath. Between the blocks, the soft rock wears away to leave the hard-topped areas standing high as hills and mountains. You can re-create the effect with a tray of sand, a watering can with a fine spray, and some coins.

1 Smooth the sand, which is soft rock, into a large, flattish mound in the middle of the tray. Place the coins here and there, and press them into the sand so they are horizontal. These are the hard-rock "caps."

2 Lightly sprinkle water from the can, as "rain." It wears away sandy, soft rock, but hard-rock coin caps protect the sand below from erosion. Gradually, valleys appear, leaving hills topped by rock caps.

31

Layers of Mountain Life

All plants need sunlight, water, warmth, and minerals to survive. But some prefer damp, shady positions while others like a dry, sunny spot. Some grow best in limey, well-drained soils; others thrive in heavy, clay soils. All these types of plants can find a home somewhere on a mountain's sides.

The plant life in the valleys is much the same as that of the surrounding area, although valleys on the leeward side of a mountain are usually drier. The influence of the mountain on the local weather (see page 12) makes the foothills moist, and the vegetation here is usually thick and lush. Farther up the slopes, as conditions become cooler, windier, and generally harsher, only trees that can survive the cold remain. Low-growing plants cling to the slopes above the trees. Ice and snow take over at the snow line and, above this, almost nothing can live.

Lower slopes
Water floods and flows more slowly on the lower slopes than on those higher up. The soil is not washed away as easily, and so it keeps its nutrients.

Valley
Soil is formed from rock particles produced by weathering, mixed with bits of dead plants and animals. In the valleys, eroded rock is washed down from the slopes, and the soil is thick. It can support the roots of large trees.

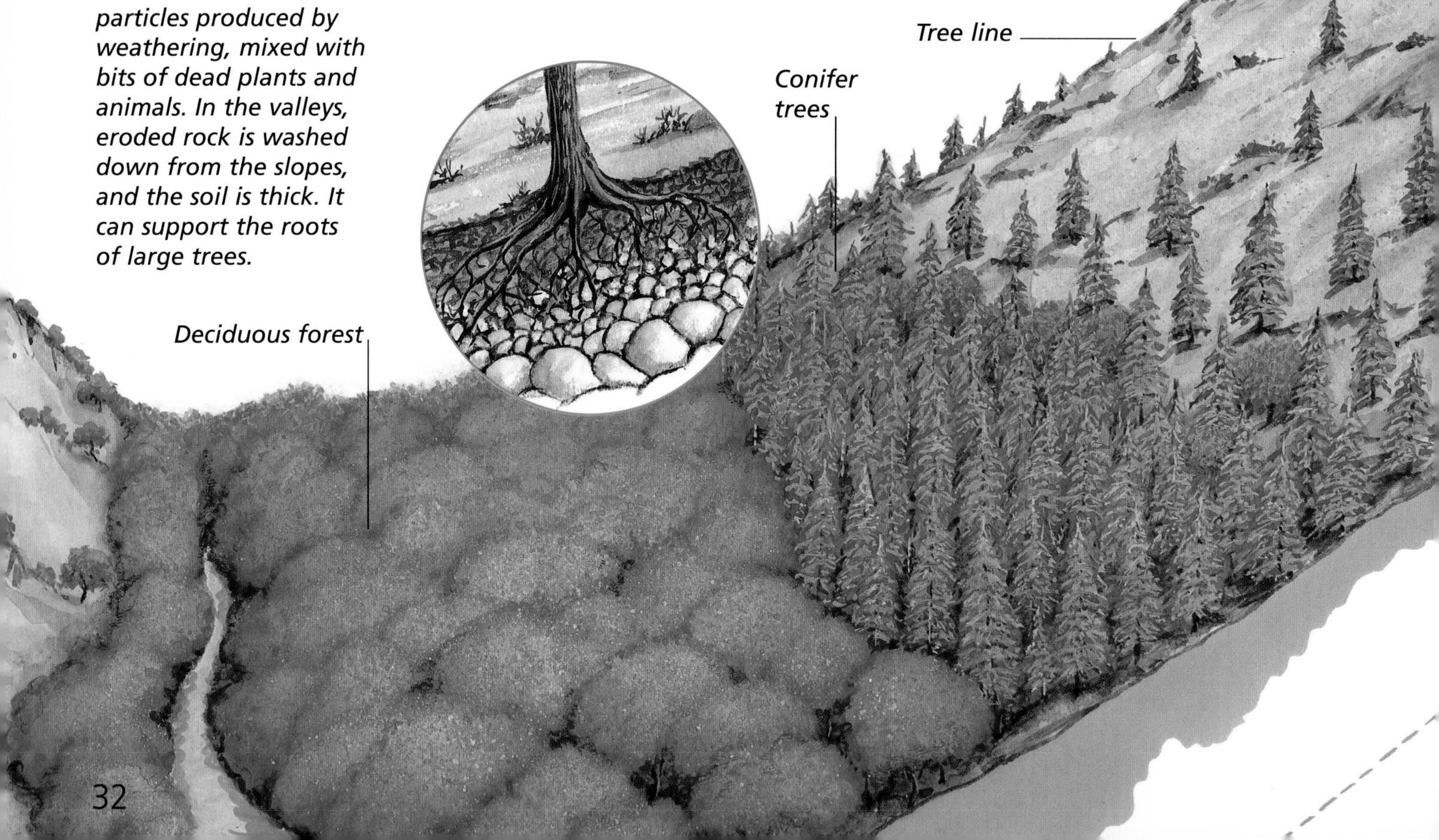

Tree line

Conifer trees

Deciduous forest

Snowy summit

Snow line

Scree slopes

Alpine meadows

Near the top
Temperatures rarely go high enough to melt the snow and ice. Hardly anything can survive on the snow and ice fields above the snow line.

Upper slopes
The fast-flowing water from higher up rushes down the steep slopes and washes away much of the soil. There is only a thin layer among the bare stones and boulders.

Plants are the first colonizers of new mountains, as their seeds blow in from afar. With luck, the seeds will grow in the bits of dust and rock-forming thin soil in pockets, cracks, and crevices. Their roots help to hold a layer of protective soil which covers the rock, soaking up water and slowing erosion. Plant roots, stems, leaves, and fruits provide food and shelter for the animals that live on the mountain.

AROUND THE WORLD

In the northern hemisphere, the north slope of a mountain is shaded from the sun for much of the time by the mountain itself. In the southern hemisphere, the same happens on south-facing slopes. The shady side is much cooler than the sunny side. This means the plants and animals living on each side of a mountain may be quite different. However, in the tropics, the sun is high overhead for more of the day, so it shines on all slopes more equally. There is less difference in the conditions, and therefore in the wildlife, between the north and south slopes.

Life near the Summit

The arctic conditions at the summits of the tallest mountains prevent any plants from growing. Often there is permanent snow and ice covering the ground. Any weathered particles are washed away by the meltwater as the snow and ice thaw, so soil does not form. But surprisingly, there is some life here. The individual microscopic cells of a type of simple plant, a red alga, live between the snowflakes just below the surface of the snow.

They are red to protect themselves from the fierce ultraviolet light from the sun that shines through the thin air at high altitudes, and could cause intense sunburn. The red color also absorbs heat from the sunshine, melting a film of thin water around the algal cell, which it can then use.

Summit conditions
Howling winds and intense cold make summit life almost impossible. But a few plants and microbes survive, on scraps and nutrients blown up from the lower slopes.

WHERE THE HARDY SURVIVE

Lichens are neither plants nor fungi, but a combination of both. They are partnerships of simple plants, called algae, and molds or fungi which are related to mushrooms and toadstools. The long, thin, microscopic cells of the fungus twine themselves around and among the green cells of the algal plant. There are hundreds of kinds of lichens. They grow where few other things can live, such as on the boulders and rocky slopes high on mountains.

Alpine clubmoss
The clubmosses are relatives of ferns and true mosses, growing to about 12 inches in height. Their stems are clothed in small leaves, and their wiry roots search out cracks and crevices.

Cladonia lichen
Sometimes called "pixie cups," this lichen grows as tiny funnels that carpet stony areas. Lichens grow very slowly, thriving in the clean, mountain air. They dislike air pollution.

The algal cells also contain special natural chemicals called "photosynthetic pigments." As in other plants, these capture the energy in sunlight, so the plant can live, grow and make its own food. The red algal cells even contain a natural "anti-freeze" so that they do not freeze solid and burst. And they can move up through the snow, by rowing themselves with tiny hairs, to get nearer the spring sunshine. Red algae can make a snowy mountain summit blush. Other plants that live high on the mountain slopes are various kinds of mosses and clubmosses. They survive under the blanket of snow in the winter. This blanket thaws in the summer, so allowing warmth and sunlight to reach the plants.

Clubmoss spores
Plants such as ferns, horsetails, and clubmosses do not grow flowers. Instead they have small, brownish capsules containing tiny spores, which look like fine dust. In a clubmoss, the male spores are much smaller than the female ones.

The moving snow line
The snow line moves down in winter, as cold grips the mountainside. A layer of snow covers the small, hardy plants. But this is helpful, since the snow acts as a blanket to keep out the worst of the wind and frost.

35

Alpine Meadows

Meadows of alpine plants grow in the zone below the snow line. The slopes here have a thin covering of soil, brought down by mountain streams from the higher areas. After the snow thaws in the spring, the alpine meadows enjoy short but sunny summers, with baking daytime temperatures and cool nights. Yet, during the short summer, meadows soon become carpeted with brightly colored flowers.

The plants must attract insects quickly in order to spread their pollen so that they can make cold-resistant seeds before winter closes in again.

In the autumn, the fierce, cold winds and snows return, and the winters are long and bleak. Plants such as hyacinths, irises, tulips, and gentians survive the winter, but they do not show above ground. They exist underground as bulbs or corms, storing enough food to enable them to sprout flowers early in the spring.

Alpine plants use many ways of keeping warm. The leaves, stems, and flowers of the edelweiss of the Alps are covered with an insulating layer

Alpine snowbell
During the short summer, this flower stores food in its roots. It uses this store to warm and melt the spring snow, so that its ready-formed flower buds can burst at the earliest moment.

Alpine cushions
Low clumps of plants dot the alpine meadow. There may be one plant type only or a mixture of species. The cushion shape gives protection from cold and wind.

Edelweiss
The hair or fur on the leaves of this plant helps to cut down water loss in the strong, drying winds. The hairy leaves also keep out the cold, like an animal's fur coat.

of hair. Most alpine plants, such as saxifrages, grow in cushions—low mounds of tightly packed leaves, well insulated against the freezing wind. In New Zealand's mountains, cushions of plants reach several feet across. Each has many different species, all growing to exactly the same height. Keeping close to the ground is a good way to avoid the wind. The snow willow of the Arctic and the high Rocky Mountains is a tree, but it is one of the smallest trees in the world. To avoid the cold wind, its twig-sized branches and tiny leaves do not rise more than a few inches above the rock face.

MOUNTAIN GIANTS

Some alpine plants have become giants rather than dwarves. Larger bodies get cold more slowly than smaller ones. The Ruwenzori Mountains of Africa sport giant groundsels over 12 feet tall. Their leaves are covered in insulating felt, which closes over the central bud at night to protect it from the cold. The saussurea (right) is a huge fluffy Himalayan daisy.

Alpine poppy
The bright yellow flowers of the alpine poppy show up well against the dark leaves, which attract insects for pollination.

Mountain Trees

Conifers—trees such as firs, spruces, pines, and larches—are well adapted to cold conditions. Their conical shape and downward-sloping branches allow the snow to slide off before it becomes too heavy and damages the tree. Most conifers (except some larches) are evergreen, which means they do not lose their leaves in winter. So they can continue to use sunlight to make energy whenever the sun shines, even in winter.

Trees like oaks, ashes, beeches, and chestnuts grow nearer the base of the mountain, where conditions are warmer and usually damper.

They are deciduous, which means they lose their leaves at a certain time each year. Deciduous trees produce harder wood than conifers. Their broad, flat leaves are efficient at gathering sunlight. But these broad leaves also lose more water into the air than the long, thin needles of conifers, so they

Silver fir
A common tree of the European Alps and Pyrenees, this fir can reach more than 165 feet high.

Paper birch
Most birches have white or silvery bark that peels off in large pieces. The paper birch's bark is like thin cardboard.

Norway spruce
Familiar as one type of "Christmas tree," this conifer—like several others—is grown in plantations for softwood timber.

Juniper
These are small trees. Their ripe, female cones resemble blue berries.

Chilean pine (monkey puzzle)
The Andes Mountains are the original home of this species. It is now grown as a decorative or ornamental tree in many regions.

Winter's bark
This broad-leaved or flowering tree bears its blossom in distinctive white clusters.

Scots pine
This pine thrives not only in Scotland, but also on light, acidic soils across Europe, north and west Asia, and North America.

Rowan
Also called the mountain ash, this broad-leaved tree bears bright red berries as fruits.

fall off when the tree shuts down its life processes for the winter. The fallen leaves rot and contribute to a rich soil, which the strong roots hold together, so other plants can grow among them.

In tropical mountains, the deciduous forest may be replaced by montane rainforest or cloud forest. Here the warm, moist conditions allow luxuriant growth of huge trees, tree ferns, creepers, and climbers, their tops 100 feet above the ground.

CONIFER TREES

Conifer trees are well adapted to the long, cold winters of the far north and south—and the same conditions on mountains. Their thin, tough needles do not dry out or wither in the cold wind, so they can stay on the tree all year. But fallen conifer needles are slow to rot in the soil, so little else grows on the ground among these trees. Conifers produce their seeds in woody cones, instead of flowers as in broad-leaved trees. Dry weather curls the cone scales back, releasing the seeds.

Older cone open to release seeds

Thin, needle-shaped leaves

Young, closed cone

Less Air, Less Pressure

As you climb up a mountain, the air gets thinner. This means air pressure or atmospheric pressure falls (see page 10). Atmospheric pressure is measured by a barometer. Mountaineers may carry a small version to measure their altitude, or height above sea level. You can make a simple barometer using a tall, thin, clear plastic bottle, a bowl of water, Scotch® tape, pen, and paper.

1 Half fill the bowl with water. Fill the bottle completely to the top with water. Put your hand firmly over its mouth and hold it there.

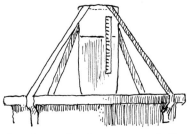

2 Tip the bottle upside down. Put its mouth in the bowl of water. Take your hand away. Some water comes out of the bottle, then it stops.

3 Tape the bottle upright in the bowl using Scotch® tape, like a big-top circus tent. Draw a measuring scale on a paper strip—say, one line every $1/4$ inch—and tape it upright on the bottle.

4 As atmospheric pressure falls with the changing weather, it presses less on the surface of the water in the bowl. This lets slightly more water out of the bottle, so the level in the bottle falls.

5 As atmospheric pressure rises, it pushes harder on the water in the bowl. This forces more into the bottle, so the water level in the bottle rises.

6 Look at the level each morning and evening, measure it on the scale and note your results. How do they compare to the weather?

7 If you could take your home-made barometer up a mountain, you would notice that the same thing happens. The water level in the bottle gradually falls as you get higher, due to the fall in atmospheric pressure.

Barometers can be used to forecast the weather.
- If the atmospheric pressure is high and steady, then fine, clear weather is likely.
- If it is low and steady, cloudy weather and rain are probable.
- If the pressure goes up and down, the weather is likely to change.

More Height, More Wind

The activity on page 15 shows how wind speed increases with height. You can measure this effect on a windy day. You need a good kite with a long, strong line, adhesive labels, pen and paper, and weighing scales of the spring-stretching type, where you put the object in a hanging pan or hang it from a hook.

When you fly a kite, always do so in the open. Beware of obstructions such as trees, buildings, and especially electricity wires, power lines or similar. Always keep at least 200 yards away from any power lines at all times.

1 The kite line should be wound around a handle that you can hook onto the scales. Unwind the line and stick written labels onto it every 10 yards.

2 Choose a day when the wind is fairly strong and steady, but not too strong, or gusty. Launch the kite and wind out the line so it flies steadily.

3 Unwind the line to the first adhesive label. Hook the handle onto the scales and measure the average pulling strain caused by the wind. Keep your fingers through the handle in case it slips off the hook!

4 Repeat step 3 until you have unwound the whole line. Note each reading on the weighing scale. Ask a friend to draw a diagram showing the angle between the kite line and the ground, so you can measure it later.

5 Wind in the kite, taking the readings again as a double-check. Back at home or in the classroom, draw a scale diagram of the kite and its line at the correct angle to the ground, on a sheet of squared paper. Measure the height of the kite for each wind-strain reading.

6 Draw a graph showing how wind speed, as indicated by the weighing scales, is affected by height. Does the wind speed go up by regular amounts? Can you calculate how fast the wind might be on a mountain 2,000 yards high, or 10,000 yards?

Bamboo Forests

Mountains in tropical parts of Asia and Africa have bamboo forests on their foothills. Most species of bamboo thrive in such warm, moist conditions. But some grow high up on the Andes and Himalayas, near the snow line, where they survive in freezing conditions. Bamboos are types of grass—the largest grasses in the world. They grow up to 100 feet tall in dense thickets. This plant lengthens at an incredible rate, up to 3 feet in two days. The long narrow leaves grow from the hollow stems, or canes, at thickenings called "nodes."

Fussy eaters

The giant panda eats bamboo and little else. Although the plant gives them all they need, the pandas have to eat large quantities for many hours each day. They have a special, extra "thumb" on each hand to help them grasp the canes and strip off the leaves. In the wild, pandas generally live as solitary animals. Because their diet is so limited, they are very vulnerable to change. Many areas of hillside bamboo forests in south-west China have been cleared for farming and dwellings, and so the pandas' habitat is shrinking.

Like other grasses, bamboo grows new plants from underground runners, but it only flowers at the end of its life. Some kinds live for more than a hundred years—then all the shoots of all the plants of that species, wherever they are, flower together and set seed, and die.

The bamboo forests of southwestern China are home to one of the world's rarest animals, the giant panda. Less than a thousand wild pandas are left, despite great efforts to save them. Bamboo has also been used by people for thousands of years, for scaffolding, boats, musical instruments, water pipes, and eating utensils such as chopsticks.

43

Threats to Mountains

Mountains were once covered in forest from their bases right up to the tree line. But today farmers and loggers have cut down the lower trees to grow crops and sell the wood. Because there are no longer tree roots to hold the soil, it is washed away. The land may become useless, so the farmers and loggers move farther up.

The water running down the mountain carries the washed-away soil with it, which chokes the fields in the valleys below. Every year, about 7,000 million cubic feet of soil are washed down from the Himalayas by the River Ganges, out into the Bay of Bengal. As methods of farming and

Logging
Huge vehicles strip trees of their branches and drag or carry the trunks to loading areas. This usually damages fragile soil.

44

terracing improve, farmers can grow crops higher up the slopes. Foresters are planting trees that cling to steeper mountainsides. Gradually the wildlife is being restricted to higher, remoter areas.

Also, many people today wish to use mountainous areas for sports and leisure. They like to go climbing, hill-walking, rock-scrambling, skiing, mountain-biking, and motorcycling. To make access and travel easier, roads and paths are cut across the slopes, and chair-lifts and mountain railways crisscross the scene. Hotels and hostels are built ever higher.

Tourists, sightseers, artists, photographers, and many others come for the scenery, peace, and solitude—yet these are becoming increasingly rare. As these activities get more popular, they do further damage. Rockfalls and avalanches pose great dangers, and speed up erosion. Mountains and their wildlife need our protection from all these threats.

Climbing
The hands, knees, and boots of climbers erode the rock and scrape bits away. Pins and spikes hammered into the stone cause cracks and flakes that speed natural erosion.

Walking and biking
The fairly recent pastime or sport of mountain-biking has caused great damage to a few upland areas. Some people show little respect for the beauty of the area or its plants and creatures.

45

Valleys for Agriculture

As the rivers and glaciers gouged out valleys, they left behind rock fragments, bits of dead leaves and plants, and the remains of dead animals and their droppings, carried down from the slopes above. These deposits gradually formed fine, fertile soils in the valleys, watered constantly by streams running down the mountainsides from high above. Many valleys are also sheltered and warm, and so they are ideal for growing crops. For thousands of years, mountain valleys have been havens for farming communities. Higher up on the steeper slopes, the soil and water can be trapped by terracing. People in East and South-East Asia have been shaping the mountain slopes for thousands of years, growing rice and other crops in flooded, perfectly level terraces wrapped around the hills and lower mountain slopes.

However, some modern agricultural methods are destroying the world's valley farms. A "Green Revolution" has bred crops that give greater yields, for extra production, to feed the millions of hungry people in the world. But these varieties need extra fertilizers, which cannot be bought by most farmers due to their high cost. The crops are treated with fertilizers and pesticides. These get into the soil and water, find their way down the slopes, and upset the balance of life in the valleys.

Terraces
Traditional terraced areas, especially in East and South-East Asia, have been producing foods such as rice for centuries. The land is levelled in strips, with walls to keep in the soil and water.

Valley bottoms
Some water trickles slowly through the terraces and irrigates the lower, flatter fields.

When Hills are Washed Bare

On the steep slopes of hills and mountains, the rain forms fast-running currents that wash away any loose material. If bushes, trees, and other plants can gain a hold, their roots work as sponges to absorb the rainwater, and as tangled nets to collect soil around them (see page 32).

When loggers remove the trees, the bare soil is not held back and it soon gets swept away. You can show this happening with a rough wooden board, fine garden soil, a fine-spray watering can, cotton balls, drinking straws, glue, and colored card.

1 Make some trees for your mountain slope. Their roots are egg-sized cotton balls, and their trunks are drinking straws pushed into the cotton balls. Their branches and leaves are cut-out card, perhaps triangular shapes to represent conifer trees like firs, glued to the straws.

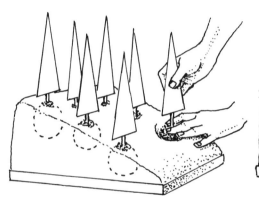

2 Put a layer of soil on the board and prop this at an angle of about 20°, to make a mountain slope. "Plant" the trees in the soil by their cotton-ball roots, making sure the cotton ball rests on the wooden board below.

3 Here comes the rain—gently sprinkle water from the can over the slope. See how the soil soaks up the water. The cotton-ball tree roots, which hold lots of water, also collect small soil particles as they are washed down.

4 The slope is logged for lumber —so remove the trees and their roots. Now make it rain again. The soil is not held back. It is soon swept down into the valley below, leaving bare hillside where plants and animals can no longer survive.

Terraces on the Slopes

When you are in a hilly area, look for evidence of terraces where the land has been flattened into a series of step-like shelves, as shown opposite.

The terraces may still be in use for agriculture, or they may have fallen into disuse because the soil has lost its nutrients, or the strips are too narrow to farm with modern equipment. Old stone walls, piled-up fences of tree trunks, or earthen ramparts show where the land was once terraced.

The same methods are used to hold up the sides of a deep, steep-sided cutting for a road, highway, or railroad line. Otherwise, rain washes the soil and plants down the steep slope, which may then collapse in a landslide.

Mountain Plant-eaters

Few animals can survive in the cold, thin air at the tops of mountains, where there are no plants to eat. The record-holders for the highest creatures are all invertebrates, or animals without backbones—mainly insects and spiders. On the desolate snow fields, thousands of tiny springtails gather to feed on the red algae. These wingless insects also survive on edible bits and pieces blown up from the lower slopes by the wind.

Lower down on the alpine meadows, when the flowers appear in the spring, surprisingly large numbers of insects swarm about to feed on their nectar, pollen, and seeds. They include butterflies, moths, beetles, and bugs of all colors, shapes, and sizes, attracted by the colorful flowers. As they feed, they help to spread the pollen which fertilizes the seeds. Caterpillars, mountain grasshoppers, and locusts chew on the leaves and stems. Some of these insects have spent the winter tucked away in some crevice, sleeping through the cold. Others have

Mountain grasshopper
Grasshoppers eat not only grass, but also the leaves, buds, shoots, and stems of the flowers and herbs in alpine meadows. With their powerful jaws, they cut through shoots and stems with ease.

Alpine longhorn
The long "horns" of this beetle are antennas, or feelers, for groping through the tangled stems and roots of the alpine pasture.

Apollo

Protected by law in many areas, this beautiful mountain butterfly can survive at heights of up to 9,800 feet. It spends the winter as a tiny caterpillar still unhatched inside its egg.

Scotch argus caterpillar

Found in grassy areas up to 6,500 feet, this caterpillar becomes a hard-cased chrysalis (pupa) and then a brown butterfly with red eyespots on its wings.

Burnet moth

Burnets are unusual for moths, because they fly in the day. Their bright colors warn predators not to eat them. This type of defence would not work at night!

survived as eggs or pupae (chrysalises), hatching as soon as the spring sun warmed them. Many high-mountain insects are dull-colored in greys, browns, and blacks. These dark hues help their bodies to absorb the weak warmth from the sunshine, and also protect them from the sun's harmful ultraviolet rays. The purple alpine longhorn beetle and the green beetle of Central Asia also use their colors as camouflage, to hide among the flowers and leaves, away from insect-eating birds. The red and black colors of the burnet moth warn that it is poisonous, so it is best left alone.

Turtle bug

Shieldbugs are a huge group of plant-chewing and sap-sucking insects. Many have bright, metallic colors.

Mountain Birds

Himalayan snowcock
One of the highest-dwelling of all birds, the Himalayan snowcock has thick feathers for warmth. Its plumage matches the patchy snow and light-colored rocks.

Small birds find mountain life hard. It is difficult to keep a small body warm, compared to a large body, and the strong winds make flying and even walking dangerous for a lightweight creature. So most small birds keep close to the ground. In the Andes Mountains of South America, flocks of diuca finches huddle tightly together under rocks to keep warm through the cold night. Nearby, the ground tyrant digs a cosy nest burrow with its beak and claws, where it shelters and also raises its chicks.

Many birds migrate south or north each autumn, to warmer climates for the winter, returning to feed and raise young next spring. A similar migration occurs on mountains, but it is vertical, or up and

American dipper
Dippers feed in mountain streams, pecking among the stones and boulders for insects such as stonefly larvae and other tasty morsels. They can walk under the water, gripping the slippery rocks with their strong feet. They use the water current flowing over their sloping backs and tails to keep them pressed down to the stream bed.

Snowfinch

Flocks of snowfinches spend their summer at heights of more than 16,400 feet. They come down to lower slopes in winter, and gather tamely around human dwellings.

Andean hillstar

This tiny bird beats its wings so fast that they make a humming sound—it is a type of hummingbird. Its long beak probes into deep, trumpet-shaped flowers for nectar.

Sword-billed hummingbird

The enormously long and thin yet lightweight beak of this small bird reaches into the narrowest and deepest of alpine flowers.

down the mountain. The birds nest and breed in the brief summer high on the slopes, taking advantage of the flowers and insects as food. Then they fly down the mountains in autumn, to shelter among the trees in the valleys for the winter.

A few birds do stay high on the mountain and endure the cold, as they have adapted to live on snow fields. They have thick, downy feathers under the main outer feathers, for extra insulation. Their legs and feet are covered with feathers too, for warmth and to act as snowshoes. When the weather gets too cold, they snuggle into the shelter of a snowdrift and go into a hibernation-like sleep. Their body processes slow down to save energy, until they are roused by a short, warmer spell.

Rock dove

An inhabitant of rocky uplands, cliffs, and gorges, the rock dove is a swift and acrobatic flier. From this wild bird have come the domestic and feral pigeons seen in towns and cities throughout the world.

Small Mammals

Red panda
The quiet red panda lives between 6,560 and 9,840 feet in the bamboo forests of the Himalayas. At night it feeds in family groups on leaves and shoots. It sleeps curled high in a tree branch during the day.

Many small mammals feed on the scarce plant life of the mountains. Some stray down to the valleys, especially during the cold of winter. One of the highest-living of all mammals is the mountain viscacha. This tough little rodent lives in the Andes Mountains, 13,000 feet above sea level. It eats grasses, mosses, and lichens. Its close relative, the chinchilla, lives slightly lower down, and has thick, silky fur to protect it from the cold.

The rock hyrax, the closest living relative of the elephant, dwells on African mountains like Mount Kenya, at altitudes of more than 9,800 feet. These hyraxes are at home on steep, rocky crags. They sun themselves by day, and huddle together in groups of 50 or more for warmth during the night.

Porcupine
The North American porcupine lives in the mixed-forest zones of North American mountain ranges. It feeds on tree buds, twigs, and bark in the winter, and flowering plants in the summer. The long, barbed quills are protection from predators.

Alpine marmot
Marmots spend the long mountain winter deep in hibernation in their burrows, huddled in family groups.

Mountain shrew
Like its lowland relations, this shrew eats insects, worms, and other small prey.

Pikas
Pikas belong to the rabbit family. They are shy and live in small groups, rarely straying from the family den in a rock crevice. They make haystacks of plant material as stores for the winter months.

Snow vole
Seeds, nuts, and other tough plant material are the snow vole's main winter food. It stays under the protective blanket of snow.

Living on Steep Slopes

Mountain animals have to cope with cold, wind, driving rain, and snow, steep and slippery slopes, and the risk of falling over a cliff or off a rock to possible death below. You can get some idea of the hazards of mountain life from these activities.

1 Try a long-jump contest and see how far you can leap. A chamois can cover 23 feet in one bound, from a standing start—and land safely on a pinnacle of rock the area of a dinner plate.

2 Have a high-jump competition at school or up some safe steps. How high can you leap? A mountain lion can spring 13 feet straight up, without a starting run.

3 Draw a chalk line or stretch a piece of rope on the ground. This is a narrow rock ridge. Can you crawl along it on all fours, turn around, and come back again? A mountain goat would do this without a single wobble.

To demonstrate the insulating power of thick fur, which is grown by many mountain mammals, especially in the winter, you need two plastic jars or beakers of water, a 0–212°F thermometer (plastic safety design,) and some furry material.

1 Put the two jars of water in the afternoon sun. Take the temperature of the water. Wrap one jar in the furry material.

2 As dusk falls and the air temperature drops, measure the temperature of the water again. Which jar is warmer?

Mountain Gorillas

Gorillas are great apes, and among our closest living relatives. There are only a few thousand left in Africa. Most are lowland gorillas. Only a few hundred are mountain gorillas, dwelling in tiny patches of highland forest up to about 12,500 feet in Rwanda and Zaïre. They have longer fur and teeth than their lowland cousins, and seem better suited to life in the cooler, high-altitude woods.

Mountain gorillas may not live so high through choice—much of the forests on the foothills has been destroyed, forcing them to the upper slopes. Gorillas live in groups of about five to twenty, consisting of females, their offspring of different ages, and one large, strong, adult male.

A quiet life
Gorillas feed mainly on leaves, also some fruit, flowers, bark, shoots, and roots. They may eat soil and their own droppings for extra minerals and vitamins. They rarely drink, but when they do, they scoop up the water and lick it from their fingers. The group feeds mainly in the mornings. In the afternoons, they travel to a new area, and at night they sleep in leafy nests.

Known as the "silverback" from the silver fur on his back, this male leads and defends the group. Like all the adults, he plays with the babies, cuddling them and allowing them to pull his fur and fingers. But if a threat appears, he rears up to his full height of 5.5–6 feet, roars loudly at the enemy, waves branches, and beats his chest. If this fails, he may charge fiercely. However, gorillas are generally peaceful creatures, spending most of their time munching leaves, resting and sleeping, and grooming each other to pick flies, ticks, lice, and other pests from the fur and skin. They are extremely threatened by the destruction of their habitat and by poachers who kill them for "trophies."

55

Browsers and Grazers

Large, herbivorous (plant-eating) mammals living on mountains have to keep on the move to avoid the worst conditions, find food and unfrozen water, and avoid predators. They must be sure-footed and agile, able to leap and run along steep slopes.

Marco Polo sheep of Turkestan trot along sharp crags and slippery scree slopes without hesitation. The African klipspringer has tiny, pointed hooves, like a ballet dancer. It can leap a 10-foot gap and land on a patch of rock the size of your hand.

The chamois of the Pyrenees and Alps has shock-absorbing legs and rubbery hoof pads for extra grip. It can jump 30 feet up sheer rock faces. Its American relative, the Rocky Mountain goat, has hollows under its hooves that work like suction cups to hold the rock. Dall's sheep in North America are much too nimble to be caught by wolves, unless they are very old or very young.

Valuable furs and wools come from these large-mammal mountain herbivores, such as the alpaca of South America (a cousin of the camel) and the angora goat. The mountain goat has a double layer of thick, white fur, as well as a thick layer of fat under its skin, to keep out the cold. The thin air makes breathing and getting oxygen difficult, so this goat has a much larger heart and more blood in its body than goats that live in the lowlands, to take in extra oxygen and spread it around the body more efficiently. Dall's sheep and Tibetan yaks have dark coats to absorb the

Chamois
The shy chamois, most agile of mountain herbivores, lives in high mountains in Europe and Western Asia. It browses on any vegetation, and can survive for two weeks without food.

Mountain goat
Found in many mountainous areas of North America, this caprid (goat-antelope) has huge hooves and long, thick fur. It moves with ease up almost-sheer cliffs and glaciers.

Klipspringer
This dwarf antelope from Africa lives in family groups and leaps with a bouncing motion over rocky outcrops.

warmth of the sun. The yak is the highest-living large mammal, grazing on lichens at altitudes of 19,700 feet. It moves down to the snow-covered alpine meadows in winter, to uncover plants for food. Yaks have long silky hair that forms a "skirt" to keep the legs warm. Most yaks are domesticated by local herdspeople, but they interbreed with the few remaining wild animals.

UPS AND DOWNS

Large animals that feed on plants often migrate to new pastures for each season. On mountains, this usually means a vertical migration. Mountain goats follow the snow line as it moves up the mountain in spring and down again in autumn. They dig up and nibble the roots and bulbs of alpine plants. The ibex, a wild goat of Europe and Asia, may descend 6,650 feet as winter approaches. It prefers steep, south-facing slopes where there is less snow during the cold months; some ibex even shelter in the forest zone below the tree line. Ibex also move down a few hundred feet each night to avoid the worst of the frost, then move up again next morning to feed.

Mouflon
A rare, wild sheep from Europe and Western Asia, the mouflon has an exceptionally woolly coat. It dwells in uplands, mountain areas, and deserts, and survives by eating almost any plant food.

American bighorn
The strongly built bighorn, a type of wild sheep, lives up to its name. It is found in the mountains and deserts of western North America. Bighorns wander with the seasons to find food wherever they can.

Vicuña
A cousin of the camel and llama, the vicuña inhabits the alpine grasslands of the Andes, up to 15,700 feet. It is about the size of a domestic sheep, but much more lightly built.

Surviving on Mountains

Hill-walking, rock-scrambling, and mountain-climbing can be amazing and exciting experiences, with spectacular views and wildlife. But they can also be deadly. Each year, dozens of people are injured or die on the high slopes of mountains. Make sure that you are properly prepared and equipped before you venture up the slopes. In a few minutes, the weather can turn from warm and sunny to cold, driving rain or fog that blots out the way to safety.

Clothes
Purpose-made walking or climbing boots and spare socks are a must. Wear loose legwear, not tight trousers that can chafe and let out body warmth. Much heat is lost through the head, so take a warm hat. You may also need sunscreen lotion.

Never go alone
Always travel in a group, preferably at least four people. If one is injured, another can stay with him/her while the others get help. One member of the group should know the area, and be familiar with survival techniques and basic first aid.

Equipment
Carry standard equipment, including extra layers of warm clothing, waterproof outer garments, a survival body-bag (plastic or foil), compass, large-scale maps, whistle, flashlight, and food rations. A mobile phone may be helpful. Use an approved backpack that leaves both arms free.

Plan and tell others
Do not make your trip too ambitious; most hill-walkers cover about 1.3 miles per hour. Check the latest weather forecasts. Leave information about where you are going and when you expect to return with the local climbing center, ranger, or camping site.

In case of emergency
Discuss and agree a plan of action. The most able and experienced should go for help. Others should find shelter in case of bad conditions, but mark their site for rescuers, using colorful clothing as a flag and arranging rocks and sticks into arrow patterns. The international distress signal is six whistle blasts or flashlight flashes, a minute's gap, then six more, and so on.

58

Mountain Hunters

Despite the desolate conditions on the tops of mountains, there is food even above the snow line. The fierce mountain winds blow a constant "rain" of tiny animals up from the valleys below. However, this food supply is usually only sufficient for small, carnivorous (meat-eating) creatures such as insects. On the Rocky Mountains, it is eaten by grylloblattids. These strange, wingless insects look like a cross between a grasshopper and a cockroach, and they are found nowhere else. Mites, beetles, and flies also feed on the rain of tiny carcasses.

Flying in the strong winds of high altitudes is difficult and dangerous for small creatures, so most mountaintop insects have no wings, or do not use them. Spiders are successful hunters from the tops to the bottoms of mountains, preying on crawling insects and trapping the flying ones in their webs. These small creatures are food for birds and small mammals who venture to the great heights.

Ladybugs
These carnivorous beetles survive the winter as adults, crammed together under rocks. They are protected from the freezing wind by each other and the snow layer over them.

Grylloblattid
Little changed since prehistoric times, this curious insect must live in near-freezing temperatures, since warmth kills it! Grylloblattids live on the glaciers, ice fields, and snowy slopes of North America's Rockies.

Earwig
Very similar in looks and habits to its valley-dwelling cousins, the mountain earwig is a scavenger. It survives on the windblown scraps of plant and animal matter.

Predatory Birds

Birds can fly long distances to find their food, whether it is insects or larger animals. So they have an advantage in mountains, being able to swoop quickly up and down the slopes, and fly to sheltered valleys when the weather worsens. The alpine chough holds the record for the highest roost of all birds, 23,000 feet up in the Himalayas near Mount Everest! Asian penduline tits have long bills for picking insects from upland plants. They cling to the stems with their long claws so the wind cannot blow them away. The alpine accentor does not often fly, but it can hold on to bare rock as it searches for insects, snails, grass seeds, and berries, venturing right up to the snow line. It crushes its food with special, strong muscles in its throat.

Andean condor
The Andean condor lives in remote areas in South America. Its numbers are still reasonably high, despite being hunted and poisoned—unlike the Californian condor, which is extremely endangered.

Peregrine
This falcon lives around the world and in many habitats, although persecution has driven it from many lowland areas into the mountains. It swoops and dives on its bird prey in mid-air.

Griffon vulture
Found across Africa, Asia, and Europe, the griffon vulture nests in the alpine grassland at over 13,000 feet. But it feeds lower in the conifer zone and shelters from the winter in deciduous trees. It scavenges on the kills of bears and wolves, picking the bones clean.

Golden eagle
Perched on a mountain crag, or soaring effortlessly on high, the golden eagle is a bird of great power. It may swoop low to hunt rabbits, hares, birds such as ptarmigans, and even reptiles and fish.

Lammergeier
A type of vulture, the lammergeier feeds on the marrow in bones left by griffon vultures. It picks them up, flies to a great height, and then drops them to smash open on the rocks. It then picks and licks out the jelly-like marrow.

Chough
The crow-like alpine chough feeds on worms, insects, and caterpillars that it draws out from under stones and crevices. It also takes berries and scavenges around human dwellings.

Larger birds need to be strong fliers to cope with the mountain winds. The great birds of prey are experts at using the rising air of up-draughts to their advantage. The huge Andean condor has a wingspan of 9 feet, and can soar for hours without flapping its wings. It looks for sick or dying animals with its sharp, long-distance eyesight. When it finds a carcass, it gorges itself so full that it cannot take off again for several hours.

Alpine accentor
About the size of your hand, this mountain-dweller is found across southern Europe, North Africa, and southern Asia, that is, from upland Spain to the Himalayas and Japan.

Small Mountain Carnivores

Compared to warm woodlands or swamps, animals of all kinds are generally scarce on mountains. So the predators that feed on other animals are even rarer. They need sharp eyes to find their prey and great agility to catch it. Many use camouflage, so that they can creep up unseen on their prey. They follow the seasonal migrations of their food up and down the mountains. Many are nocturnal—they hunt mainly at night. The Himalayan palm civet and the Cuban solenodon search for insects, mice, and other small animals in mountain forests. Lorises or bushbabies in Asian or African high rainforests use their huge eyes to find prey in the dark.

Silky anteater

The size of a small domestic cat, the silky anteater is the smallest of the four kinds of anteater. Its prehensile tail grips the branches strongly.

Pine marten

A relation of the stoat and weasel, the pine marten runs and climbs through the conifer woodlands on mountain slopes. It eats any small animals, from insects to mice, also birds and eggs.

Solenodon

Looking like a shrew, but the size of a rat, the solenodon of Cuba kills its prey with poisonous saliva. It eats small creatures among the fallen leaves.

The silky anteater lives in the trees of cloud forests in the Andes Mountains of South America, and rarely goes down to the ground. It feeds on ants and termites at night, breaking open their tree-trunk nests with its strong claws and licking out the insects with its long, sticky tongue. In Asian cloud forests, the mongoose hunts anything it can catch. In Europe the red fox adapts as well to hunting on mountains as it does to foraging in town dumpsters.

Weasels, stoats, polecats, and martens hunt on the forest slopes of mountains in Europe and North America. These shy creatures are active at any time of the day or night, whenever they spot a victim.

Bears in High Places

Some kinds of bears are adaptable enough to thrive on mountains. They are omnivores, which means they eat almost anything, plant, or animal—fruits, leaves, insects, dead and rotting flesh, eggs, honey, or fish. A typical bear has a large body which conserves heat and is well insulated with thick fur and fat under the skin. The large paws and short, strong legs help with climbing rocks or trees.

The only bear in South America is the spectacled bear, named for the markings on its face. It lives in the warm Andean rainforests, at up to 13,000 feet, feeding on plants but also hunting animals. Each evening, it makes a sleeping nest in a tree. The brown bear, also called the grizzly or kodiak bear, lives in the temperate forests and uplands of North America, Europe, and Asia.

Spectacled bear
This medium-sized bear climbs well and eats fruits such as figs. It may chase and kill young deer, vicuñas, guanacos, and similar larger animals.

Brown bear
There are many brown bears in remote regions of northern North America and northern Asia, but they are rare elsewhere, having been driven into the mountains by people.

HIBERNATION

Some mammals survive cold winters by going into hibernation in a sheltered place. This is no ordinary sleep. The heartbeat and breathing slow right down; the body becomes cold and its chemical life processes almost stop. Alpine marmots go into true hibernation for half the year. Brown bears do not. They enter a sleep called torpor, with slightly lowered body temperature, but hardly unchanged heartbeat and breathing. They often wake up if the weather turns warm.

One of its favorite foods is fresh salmon, which it catches as they swim up mountain streams. The bears fatten themselves up for their winter sleep on leaves and fruit. In some places the brown bear is becoming rare, because of persecution by people and destruction of its natural habitat.

The Asiatic black bear lives at heights of up to 11,800 feet on Himalayan mountains. It is mainly a plant-eater and sometimes raids farm crops. But, like all bears, it eats and scavenges almost anything, and occasionally it attacks farm animals.

Mountain Cats

Many kinds of wild cats, large and small, live and hunt on mountains and in valleys. Cats are usually solitary animals that patrol large home ranges. They hunt mainly other mammals and birds, by stalking them—usually at night. They rely on camouflage so that they can creep up on unsuspecting prey and pounce at the last minute. The African caracal has long tufts of hair at the ends of its ears and very long legs. It is extremely adaptable, equally at home in mountains, deserts, and woodlands. The lynx of North America, Europe, and Asia has ear and cheek tufts, but only a stumpy tail. It hunts deer, killing with a single bite at the back of the neck.

Snow leopard
As rare as it is beautiful, the snow leopard or ounce lives and hunts at about 18,000 feet in the Himalayas. It moves up and down the slopes with its prey, which ranges from mice and small birds to wild sheep, deer, and cattle.

Andean cat
Found on the Andes Mountains from Peru to Chile, this cat is also called the mountain cat. It has very thick fur and a distinctly ringed tail. It hunts in the mountain grassland, scrubland, and forest.

Wild cat
A larger version of the domestic cat, the wild cat is secretive and rarely seen. It lives across Europe and North Africa, east to India, and preys on small mammals and birds.

North American mountain lions, also called cougars or pumas, are very agile and can leap about on rocky ledges. They usually live alone in huge, overlapping ranges of hundreds of square miles, preying on deer, rabbits, and rodents. The spotted kittens are born at the end of the winter in a cave den and stay with their mother for about a year. Like several other cat species, mountain lions are endangered because they have been killed by farmers protecting their animals.

The snow leopard suffered greatly from fur trapping because of its beautiful, thick, spotted fur. The few hundred animals left in the world today live permanently high in the Himalayas, far from people. They have thick pads of fur underneath their feet, to walk on soft snow and grip ice.

The beautiful camouflage patterns on the coats of many mountain cats, and the luxurious thickness of their fur, meant that huge numbers were once killed for their skins—so that humans could wear them. This trade has lessened in recent years, but many wild cats are still rare and under threat.

Mountain lion
This medium-sized cat can survive almost anywhere. It does well in mountain regions, preying on a variety of animals from mice to deer.

Lynx
The lynx prefers thick scrub and conifer forest. It is found in the north and on mountains. This cat has large paws with thick fur to stay warm and grip the slippery rocks and ice.

FUR TRAPPING

Native peoples have used animal skins to keep themselves warm for thousands of years. But from the 1850s, people had money to buy fashionable furs. Trapping became big business. Today, the fur trade is strictly controlled. But poachers still hunt cats large and small, and sell furs for high prices.

Mountain and Valley Soils

The soils on mountains are usually shallow, thin, and poor. The soil in valleys is generally deeper and richer in nutrients. You can compare the two types of soil using a small trowel, plastic bags with labels, large clear jars, and some water.

Take care when you venture into mountains, and always go with an adult (see page 2 and 58.) Also, before you dig up any soil, you must make sure that you have permission from the landowner, and that the area is not a nature reserve or protected in any way.

1 Take a sample of soil by digging one trowelful from a site high in the mountains. Do not dig up any plants or disturb any animals. Seal the sample in the plastic bag and label it.

2 Take more samples from lower down the hillside. Obtain the last sample from low in a valley. Label them, as before. Try to make sure each sample is the same size or volume.

Mountain soil usually has lots of large or coarse pieces that are freshly broken from the rocks, and not much small or fine matter.

3 Three-quarters fill each large jar with water. Add a soil sample to each one. Stir and shake the jars vigorously, then let them settle for an hour or two.

Large particles of sand

Largest particles of small stones and just-eroded rock fragments settle first.

Bits of leaves, twigs and similar pieces float on top.

Water is hazy due to still-suspended silt which settles last.

4 Study the soil samples and record what you see. The samples probably have different-sized pieces in them. Is there a clear gradation or trend, from high soils to low ones?

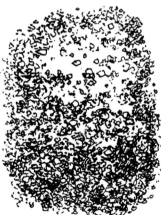

Valley soil usually has few larger particles. It is mainly small or fine material, plus lots of broken-down bits of plants.

Indicators of Pollution

Some mountains are wild and remote, with few people or dwellings, and fresh, clean air. Other mountain areas are very populated with towns, vehicles, and factories, which produce smoke, gases, and dust to pollute the air. Living things called lichens, which look like crusty plants, can show if the air is clean or dirty.

Some lichens survive in fairly polluted air, even in town centers. Other lichens are able to live only in clean air. So lichens are "natural indicators of pollution." Look for them next time you are out in the countryside. Lichens may also change as you go from the polluted air down in a valley to the clean air high in the mountains.

Clean air
Bushy lichens are usually green or grey. They only grow in clean air. Pollution kills them.

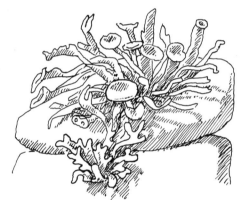

A lichen (see page 34) is a combination or partnership of two types of living things. These are a simple plant called an alga, and a fungus— a living thing from the same group as mushrooms, toadstools, and molds. The exact type of alga and fungus gives each lichen its color and shape.

Medium air
Flat, rounded lichens can cope with slight pollution. They may be yellow, black, orange, or green.

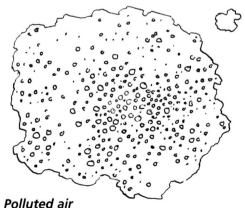

Polluted air
Crusty lichens look like dried-out slices of bread with curled edges. They are usually green or grey.

How old?
Most lichens grow very slowly. A patch the size of your hand may be a hundred years old. Look for lichens on trees and rocks, and also on old buildings, walls, and gravestones. You may be able to tell the greatest age of a lichen on a gravestone, from the dates carved on the stone.

Amazing Facts

The highest place on Earth is the summit of Mount Everest, 29,028 feet above sea level. It was first climbed by Edmund Hillary and Tenzig Norgay in 1953.

The next nine mountains in the top ten are all in the Himalaya region of south-central Asia, stretching from northern Pakistan across northern India, China, Nepal, Bhutan, and the Tibet region of China:

K2 (Godwin Austen)	28,250 feet
Kangchenjunga Main Peak	28,180 feet
Lhotse Main Peak	27,890 feet
Kangchenjunga South Peak	27,790 feet
Makalu I	27,785 feet
Kangchenjunga West Peak	27,620 feet
Lhotse East Peak	27,490 feet
Dhaulagiri	26,800 feet
Cho Oyu	26,740 feet

In fact, the Himalayas contain the top 28 tallest peaks in the world. They are still relatively young mountains, only 50 million years old, and they are rising by about 2 inches every year.

This is beaten by the lowest point on the Earth's continents—the Bentley Trench under the ice and glaciers of Antarctica, where the rock is 8,327 feet below sea level.

However, the world's tallest peak is Mauna Kea in Hawaii. From its base on the seabed to its summit, it is 33,474 feet, with the summit rising 13,795 feet above sea level.

The largest gorge in the world is the Grand Canyon in Arizona. The Colorado river flows along the bottom. The canyon's maximum depth is 5,250 feet; its width varies from 4 to 18 miles, and its overall length is about 210 miles.

The lowest point of dry land on Earth is Death Valley, California. It is 282 feet below sea level.

The tallest, active volcano is Ojos del Salado, between Chile and Argentina, at 22,600 feet high.

The highest, volcanic mountain is Aconcagua in Argentina (see top opposite.) It is extinct.

The Andes of South America is the longest mountain range at 4,700 miles.

The shores of the Dead Sea in the Middle East may be 1,300 feet below sea level, depending on the lake's water level. The deepest part of the lake bed is 2,390 feet below sea level.

The tallest peaks on each of the other main continents or landmasses are:

Aconcagua	22,835 feet	(Andes, South America)
McKinley	20,321 feet	(Alaska, North America)
Kilimanjaro	19,340 feet	(East Africa)
Vinson	16,066 feet	(Antarctica)
Blanc	15,770 feet	(European Alps)
Wilhelm	14,795 feet	(Papua New Guinea, SE Asia)
Elbert	14,432 feet	(Rockies, North America)
Cook	12,349 feet	(New Zealand)
Kosciusko	7,313 feet	(Australia)

The deepest bed of any lake or river is the bottom of Lake Baikal, Russia, at 3,875 feet below sea level.

The Yarlung Zangbo valley in the Himalayas of Tibet is the world's deepest land valley, with its floor 16,650 feet below the ridges on either side.

The deepest valley in the world is a submarine canyon—the Challenger Deep of the Mariana Trench in the northwest Pacific, at 36,160 feet below sea level.

The Vicos Gorge in Greece is the deepest narrow canyon, 3,000 feet down, yet only 3,600 feet wide.

Mount Kilimanjaro is 19,340 feet high, the highest mountain in Africa. Mount Kenya stands 17,060 feet high. They are both extinct volcanoes.

Find Out More

The best place to begin your search for more information is your school library. Another excellent source of information is your public library. Most newspapers carry regular reports of new advances in science each week. For more information about the plants and animals described in this book, check with your nearest natural history museum or wildlife refuge. They can put you in touch with your local natural history associations as well.

We have listed below a selection of books, organizations, videos, and multimedia programs that will help you learn more about MOUNTAINS AND VALLEYS.

GENERAL INFORMATION

Acid Rain Foundation
1410 Varsity Drive
Raleigh, NC 27606
919-828-9443
Adopt-a-Stream Foundation
P.O. Box 5558 , Everett, WA 98206
206-388-3313
American Forest Council
1250 Connecticut Avenue NW
Suite 320, Washington, DC 20036
202-463-2455
American Rivers, Inc.
801 Pennsylvania Avenue SE
Suite 303
Washington, DC 20003-2167
202-547-6900
American Wildlands
40 East Main Street
Suite 2,

Bozeman, MT 59715
406-586-8175
Bat Conservation International
P.O. Box 162603
Austin, TX 78716-2603
512-327-9721
Ducks Unlimited
1 Waterfowl Way
Long Grove, IL 60047
312-438-4300
Freshwater Foundation
2500 Shadywood Road
Box 90, Navarre, MN 55392
612-471-8407
Great Bear Foundation
P.O. Box 2699, Missoula, MT 59806
406-721-3009
Great Swamp Research Institute
Office of the Dean
College of Natural Sciences and Math
Indiana University of Pennsylvania
305 Weyandt Hall
Indiana, PA 15705
412-357-2609
National Audubon Society
950 Third Avenue
New York, NY 10022
212-832-3200
National Geographic Society
17th and M Streets, NW
Washington, DC 20036
202-857-7000
National Parks and Conservation
Association, 1015 31st Street NW
Washington, DC 20007
202-944-8530
National Wildlife Federation
1400 16th Street NW
Washington, DC 20036
202-797-6800
The Nature Conservancy
1815 N. Lynn Street
Arlington, VA 22209
703-841-5300
Save the Redwoods League
114 Sansome Street
Room 605, San Francisco, CA 94104
415-362-2352
Sierra Club
100 Bush Street

San Francisco, CA 94104
415-291-1600
The Wilderness Society
1400 Eye Street NW
Washington, DC 20005
202-842-3400

BOOKS

Ecology Projects for Young Scientists
Martin J. Gutnik
Franlkin Watts
ISBN 0-531-04765-2
Exploring Our Living Planet Robert D.
Ballard, National Geographic ISBN
0-87044-459-X
Science Nature Guides: Birds
Thunder Bay Press
ISBN 1-85028-261-7
Science Nature Guides: Butterflies
Thunder Bay Press
ISBN 1-57145-018-1
Science Nature Guides: Fossils
Thunder Bay Press
ISBN 1-85028-262-5
Science Nature Guides: Insects
Thunder Bay Press
ISBN 1-57145-017-3
Science Nature Guides: Mammals
Thunder Bay Press
ISBN 1-57145-016-5

VIDEOS

National Geographic Society
produces a wide range of wildlife and geographical videos
Time-Life Video
produces a wide range of wildlife and geographical videos

MULTIMEDIA

3D Atlas Electronic Arts
The Big Green Disc Gale Research
Eyewitness Encyclopedia of Nature
Dorling Kindersley
Global Learning Mindscape
Picture Atlas of the World
National Geographic Society
Survey of the Animal Kingdom
Zane Publishing
A World Alive Softline

Glossary

acid rain Rain that has acidic chemicals dissolved in it, usually from the polluting gases and vapors given off in vehicle exhausts, and by the chimneys of factories and power stations.

block-fault mountains Mountains formed when the land cracks along faults and then moves up or down, to leave a raised block that is the mountains.

carnivore An animal that eats other animals, usually a hunter that feeds on meat or flesh.

contour line On a map, a line that joins all places of the same altitude, or height above sea level. Lines close together indicate steep slopes and cliffs.

crust The outermost layer of the Earth, which is mostly solid, and which is very thin compared to the whole Earth (in proportion, it is thinner than the skin on an apple).

deciduous Trees that regularly lose or drop their leaves at a certain time of year, usually Fall or the dry season.

deforestation Cutting down or burning trees and clearing woodlands and forests for various uses, such as for the trees' timber, and to plant crops, raise farm animals, or build roads, factories, and houses.

erode/erosion Wearing away the land by physical methods such as rubbing and scraping, and carrying away the eroded results such as rock particles (see WEATHERING).

fold mountains Mountains formed when the rocks in the Earth's CRUST bend and buckle into folded shapes.

habitat A type of place or surroundings in the natural world, often named after the main plants that grow there. Examples are a conifer forest, a grassland such as a meadow, a desert, a pond, or a sandy seashore. Some animals are adapted to only one habitat, like limpets on rocky seashores. Other animals, like foxes, can survive in many habitats.

herbivore An animal that eats plant food, such as shoots, stems, leaves, buds, flowers, and fruits.

hot-spot A stationary region under the Earth's CRUST which forces up molten rocks and gases. Volcanoes occur along a line there, as the TECTONIC PLATE slides across the spot

igneous Rocks that were once so hot that they became molten or melted, then they have cooled and become solid.

lava Rocks and minerals which come out of a volcano and which are so hot that they are melted or molten, so they flow.

lithospheric plate See TECTONIC PLATE.

oceanic trench The deepest canyon-like parts of the ocean, where the seabed plunges almost vertically. It is usually formed as one TECTONIC PLATE subducts (slides) under another.

rift valley A valley formed by cracking and pulling apart of the Earth's CRUST, along a rift or fault.

strata Layers or beds of rocks, usually formed by particles settling in water to form layers of sediments.

tectonic plate One of the giant curved plates that makes up the outer surface of the Earth, that moves or drifts in relation to the other plates. (Also called a lithospheric plate.)

tor A group of slabs or boulders usually capping a hill, left behind after the surrounding land has been eroded.

tree line The edge of the woods and forests, which marks the place where the climate becomes too cold and/or dry for trees to grow.

weathering The action of sun, wind, rain, ice, and other natural activities that crack and break rocks (see EROSION).

Index